Progressive
Around the Drums with
Syncopation

by Jim Latta

90 MINUTE STEREO CASSETTE AVAILABLE

The most important exercises in
Progressive Around the Drums with Syncopation
have been recorded onto a 90 minute STEREO cassette
tape and will be a valuable aid to your progress.

** I dedicate this book to my wife
and best friend Pat. (The girl from Jersey)*

Acknowledgements
Cover: Phil Martin
Instruments supplied by John Reynolds Drum City

Distributed By

in **Australia**
Koala Publications
4 Captain Cook Ave.
Flinders Park 5025
South Australia
Ph (08) 268 1750
Fax (08) 347 4019

in **U.S.A.**
Koala Publications
3001 Redhill Ave.
Bldg. 2 # 104
Costa Mesa CA
U.S.A. 92626
Ph (714) 546 2743
Fax 1-714-546 2749

in **U.K. and Europe**
Music Exchange
Claverton Road, Wythenshawe,
Manchester M23 9NE
Ph (061) 946 1234
Fax (061) 946 1195

ISBN 0 947183 69 8

Reorder code KP-SD

Contents

(Contents continued next page)

Contents (cont.)

Introduction

Progressive "Around the Drums with Syncopation" has been designed to give drummers, of all styles and levels of playing ability, a carefully graded introduction to reading and playing drum music. The drum player is introduced to basic rhythms and then gradually introduced to syncopated rhythms using the whole drum kit.

Although a drummer can enjoy a career playing certain forms of music never having to read, it can extremely limit his playing skills. By simply learning to read and play the exercises in this book your musicianship will increase dramatically.

Jim Latta M.I.M.T.
(Member, Institute of Music Teachers)

JIM LATTA
M. I. M. T.
(Member, Institute of Music Teachers)

Jim Latta is senior lecturer in Drums and Percussion at the college for Technical and further education. He has performed with many Jazz and Pop artists including Don Burrows, Bee Gees, Shirley Bassey, John Farnham, George Golla, Pete Condoli and Frank Rosolino.
Jim also works as session musician and teacher.

Explanation of Drum Notation

Snare Drum   Small Tom Tom   Middle Tom Tom

Floor Tom Tom   Bass Drum   Hi-Hat or Cymbal

> = Accent

* Please note that stem direction is likely to alternate e.g. up ♩ or down ⌐ .

Counting Guide

Notes	Notation and Count	Say
Quarter Notes	♩ ♩ ♩ ♩ 1　2　3　4	one two three four
Eighth Notes	♫ ♫ ♫ ♫ 1 + 2 + 3 + 4 +	one and two and three and four and "and" is pronounced "an"
Eighth Note Triplets	(triplets) 3 3 3 3 1 + a 2 + a 3 + a 4 + a	one and a, two and a, three and a, four and a "a" is pronounced as "uh" Say 1 triplet, 2 triplet, 3 triplet, 4 triplet to help get the "feel" of the rhythm
Sixteenth Notes	(sixteenths) 1 e + a 2 e + a 3 e + a 4 e + a	one e and a, two e and a, three e and a, four e and a, "e" is pronounced "ee"
Eighth Note plus two Sixteenth Notes	(eighth + two sixteenths) 1 e + a 2 e + a 3 e + a 4 e + a	one-and a, two-and a, three-and a, four-and a Say boom-chucka, boom-chucka to help get the "feel" of the rhythm
Two Sixteenth Notes plus an Eighth Note	(two sixteenths + eighth) 1 e + a 2 e + a 3 e + a 4 e + a	one e and, two e and, three e and, four e and Say chucka-boom, chucka- boom, to help get the "feel" of the rhythm
Dotted Eighth Notes plus a Sixteenth Note	(dotted eighth + sixteenth) 1 e + a 2 e + a 3 e + a 4 e + a	one-a, two-a, three-a, four-a
Sixteenth Note plus Eighth Note plus a Sixteenth Note	(sixteenth + eighth + sixteenth) 1 e + a 2 e + a 3 e + a 4 e + a	one e-a, 2 e-a, 3 e-a, 4 e-a e-a pronounced "ee-uh".

Section One

The 15 Lessons in Section One use basic notation rhythms around the drums. Incorporating quarter notes, eighth notes, sixteenth notes, triplets, dotted eighth notes and combinations of each.

Approach to Practice

It is important to have a correct approach to practice. You will benefit more from several short practices e.g. 30-40 mins every day rather than one or two long sessions per week. Work your way through this book exercise by exercise. Try to read and count (aloud) each exercise, don't just play them from memory. It is very important to be able to count each exercise. If you can't count them correctly you will not be able to play them correctly. Use alternate sticking at first then use your own. Practice slowly at first and increase speed as your reading and playing ability improves. To ensure you play each rhythm correctly the audio cassette containing the exercises is highly recommended, as is the guidance of an experienced teacher.

Refer to the counting guide on the previous page before commencing each lesson.

Lesson 1

Quarter Notes (♩) Quarter Note Rests (𝄽) and Half Note Rests (▬)

16 Bar Solo Exercise

Lesson 2

Eighth Notes (♫) and Quarter Notes (♩)

16 Bar Solo Exercise

Lesson 3

Dotted Eighth Note joined to Sixteenth Note (♪. ♪) with Quarter Notes (♩)

14

16 Bar Solo Exercise

Lesson 4

Eighth Note Triplets (♪♪♪) with Quarter Notes (♩)

16 Bar Solo Exercise

Lesson 5

Eighth Note Triplets (♪♪♪) with Eighth Notes (♪♪)
etc.

16 Bar Solo Exercise

Lesson 6

Eighth Note Triplets (♪♪♪) with Dotted Eighth Notes joined to Sixteenth Notes (♪.♪)

16 Bar Solo Exercise

Lesson 7

Eighth Notes (♪♪) with Dotted Eighth Note joined to Sixteenth Note (♪.♪)

16 Bar Solo Exercise

Lesson 8

Sixteenth Notes (♫♫) and Quarter Notes (♩)

16 Bar Solo Exercise

Lesson 9

Sixteenth Notes (♪♪♪♪) and Eighth Notes (♪♪)

16 Bar Solo Exercise

Lesson 10

Sixteenth Notes (♪♪♪♪) and Dotted Eighth Note joined to Sixteenth Note (♪. ♪)

16 Bar Solo Exercise

Lesson 11

Eighth Notes joined to two Sixteenth Notes (♪♬ and ♩♬)
with Eighth Notes (♪♪) and Sixteenth Notes (♬♬)

30

32 Bar Solo Exercise

Lesson 12

Eighth Notes joined to two Sixteenth Notes (♪♫ and ♫♪)
with Dotted Eighth Note joined to a Sixteenth Note (♪.♬)

16 Bar Solo Exercise

Lesson 13

Sixteenth Note - Eighth Note – Sixteenth Note joined
as a group of three (♫ ♪) with Quarter Notes (♩)

16 Bar Solo Exercise

Lesson 14

Sixteenth Note - Eighth Note – Sixteenth Note joined
as a group of three (♪♪♪) with Eighth Notes (♪♪)

16 Bar Solo Exercise

Lesson 15

Sixteenth Note – Eighth Note – Sixteenth Note joined as a group of three (♪♫)
with Dotted Eighth Note joined to a Sixteenth Note (♪. ♫)
etc.

16 Bar Solo Exercise

Lesson 16

Sixteenth Note - Eighth Note – Sixteenth Note joined
as a group of three (♬) with Sixteenth Notes (♬♬)

Count: 1 e + a 2 e + a 3 e + a 4 e + a

16 Bar Solo Exercise

Lesson 17

Sixteenth Note – Eighth Note – Sixteenth Note joined as a group of three (♪)
with Eighth Note joined to two Sixteenth Notes (♪ and ♪)

16 Bar Solo Exercise

Lesson 18

Sixteenth Note – Eighth Note – Sixteenth Note joined as a group of three (♫) with Sixteenth Notes (♬) and Eighth Notes joined to two Sixteenth Notes (♪♬ and ♪♬) etc.

16 Bar Solo Exercise

48

32 Bar Solo Exercise

Incorporating all Exercises from Lessons Ten to Fourteen.

Section Two

The four remaining lessons in Section Two introduce basic syncopation around the drums, incorporating eighth note rests, with eighth notes, quarter notes and tied notes.

When practicing these exercises, always start *slowly* and *count* (out loud if necessary) keeping a steady even pulse with the bass drum.

The last pages in Section Two are exercises specifically designed for bass drum control. Reliable foot control is essential and these exercises will help considerably.

Lesson 19

Eighth Note Rest (𝄾) with Eighth Notes (♫) and Quarter Notes (♩)

51

32 Bar Solo Exercise

Lesson 20
Introducing Syncopation

Syncopation is the accenting of a normally unaccented beat. i.e. an "off the beat" rhythm.

e.g. a basic rhythm

a syncopated rhythm

The key to learning how to read syncopation is to learn how to **count** it correctly. Drummers more than any other instrumentalist seem to have a problem with this. Part of the reason is that few books offer drummers a complete explanation, especially for beginners.

We commence with a study of 8 eighth notes and the way they are **counted**, which is:

Counted: "and" "and" "and" "and"
           1 + 2 + 3 + 4 +

For simplification, we will refer to this as Key Number One.

Divide a bar of $\frac{4}{4}$ time into eight eighth notes.

Count 1 + 2 + 3 + 4 +

There are two eighth notes in a quarter note.
So a quarter note could be

♩ =(1+) or (2+) or (3+) or (4+)

or   ♩ = (+2) or (+3) or (+4) section of the count

An eighth note can be

♪ = (1) or (2) or (3) or (4)

or any of the "ands" (+)

A dotted note is equal to three notes half its value e.g. ♩. = ♪♪♪

Therefore a dotted quarter note (♩.) is equal to three eighth notes.

♩. = (1+2) or (+2+) or (2+3) or (+3+) or (3+4) or (+4+) section of the count.

If you wish to work out a bar of syncopation,

for example: place it under the "key" like so:

Play the bass drum on all the numbers, as a time keeper. Count out loud "**1+2+3+4+**" and play the syncopated beat.

Because of the characteristic of the instrument, drummers cannot "hang on" to a note, or play much longer than a quarter note (unless a closed roll [buzz roll] or cymbal crash is played). As a result of this, drummers may be required to read **three** ways of playing the same drum pattern.

In the 12 exercises on page 55, each bar, although written differently, sounds the same when played by a drummer.

The middle bar of each exercise incorporates tied notes. The second note of a tie is not played.

e.g. written as ♩♩♩ played as ♩♩ 𝄾

Note: The bass drum is deleted on these exercises so you can see how the syncopation is counted without the aid of a **written** bass drum.

Use page 55 as a guide, especially for the exercises on syncopation where the bass drum has been deleted.

55

Study this page carefully.
Note the **three** ways of writing the same pattern.
(For tied notes – refer page 58).

56

Play the following examples of syncopation around the drums.
Bass drum keeps a steady beat.

Tied Notes

Because drummers cannot always hold a note to its correct value, as most other instruments can, it is essential for beginners to treat the **second** note of the tie as a rest, and not to play it.
Here are some examples:

In Example (A) think of the 1st half of the 3rd beat as a rest. In Example (B) think of the 1st half of the 4th beat as a rest. In Example (C) think of the 1st half of beats 2, 3, 4 as rests.

59

24 Bar Solo Exercise

Lesson 21

Syncopation

The bass drum plays a steady 4 beats per bar (although not written). This helps you to read syncopation more effectively. The following exercises are on snare only.

32 Bar Solo Exercise

Play slowly - count aloud - alternate sticking.

Once you have completed playing exercises 354 - 385 as written go back and play them as a triplet rhythm or jazz swing feel.

To do this, we commence with a study of eighth note triplets and the way in which they are counted (refer to page 7).

e.g.: Count

We will refer to this as "Key Number Two".

You are now counting three even beats over each beat of the pulse, instead of two even beats. The rhythm of the syncopation will be played in a different position in the bar.

To analyse a bar of syncopation played as a jazz or swing feel, place it under "Key Number Two" thus:

Then play the bass drum on all the numbers. As a time keeper, count "**1+a, 2+a, 3+a, 4+a**", and play the bar of syncopation.

A study of the examples below, will help clarify this method.

Example One:

Example Three:

Example Two:

Example Four:

32 Bar Solo Exercise

386

Play slowly - count aloud - alternate sticking.

32 Bar Solo Exercise

Play slowly - count aloud - alternate sticking.

32 Bar Solo Exercise

388

Play slowly - count aloud - alternate sticking.

32 Bar Solo Exercise

389

Play slowly - count aloud - alternate sticking.

Lesson 22
Bass Drum Control for Basic Rhythms

The most common problem with beginners is co-ordination of the feet. When playing basic rhythms, it is essential to have reliable foot control. Make your hands fit in with the bass drum, not vice versa. The bass drum is the time – the pulse. It does not slow down or speed up according to the rhythm being played with your hands, it stays constant and steady. With regular practice, you come to *rely* on the bass drum for steady time, which produces a comfortable feeling with the end result of a confident, steady rhythm when you play. As you gain experience, the time can be transferred from your feet to your body, and the regular pulse is "felt" rather than actually played. This enables the experienced drummer to play rhythms within the time with the feet also, thus creating "four way" independence with the limbs. The following exercises are specifically designed for bass drum control. For further studies in independence, refer to "Progressive Rock, Jazz & Funk Drumming".

Start Slowly

Practice the following exercises with right hand on cymbal or hi-hat.